IMAGES OF ENGLAND

CLAYTON AND OPENSHAW

IMAGES OF ENGLAND

CLAYTON AND OPENSHAW

JILL CRONIN AND FRANK RHODES

The History Press

Frontispiece: A group of girls, aged about nine and from
St Clement's church, take part in a Whit Walk (*c.* 1954). On
the left is the senior day school of the church on Gransmoor
Road, Higher Openshaw. From the left are: -?- , Beverley ?, -?,
Christine Bennett (*née* Ellison), Lynne Judges and Audrey Wood.

First published in 2005 by Tempus Publishing

Rprinted in 2009 by
The History Press
The Mill, Brimscombe Port,
Stroud, Gloucestershire, GL5 2QG
www.thehistorypress.co.uk

British Library Cataloguing in Publication Data.
A catalogue record for this book is available from the British Library.

ISBN 978 0 7524 3521 3

Typesetting and origination by
Tempus Publishing.
Printed and bound in Great Britain.

Contents

Acknowledgements

We should like to thank all those who have helped us in any way and the following people, who have given kind permission for us to include their photographs: Eva Adshead, Father Stewart Ansbro of St Willibrord's church, Audenshaw Local History Society, George and Christine Bennett, Annie Buxton, the staff at Clayton Health Centre and at Clayton Library, Clayton Local History Group especially Marion Hogan, Maggie Reed and Elizabeth Wells, Janet Coles, the Co-operative Movement, Rita Deegan, Jean and David Dore, Sylvia and Albert Gregory, Tony and Helen Hannan, the late Stan Horritt, Kath Hughes, Anne Kershaw, Claire Knott, Marie Koudellas, Ken Lilley, Dorothy Lord, Peter McGarr, the Manchester Evening News, the Manchester Police Museum, Mr and Mrs M.Maxwell, the Museum of Science and Industry in Manchester, Jacqueline Oliver, Joyce and John Pemberton, Alan Rose, Joan Schofield, Lena Slack, Colin Southworth, the late Eva Turner, Harold Walton, Laura Warburton, Marie and Charlie Welsh and Lesley Worthington.

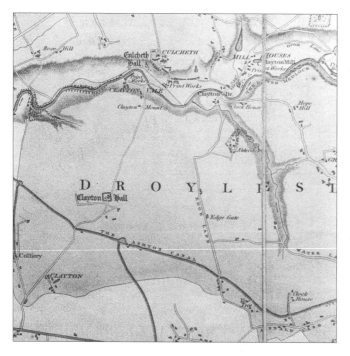

Johnson's map of 1820 showing the areas of Clayton and Openshaw. The River Medlock bounds Clayton on the north with Newton Heath and on the west with Bradford. Ashton Canal and Ashton Old Road run through a rural landscape, with just two small clusters of houses. Clayton Hall (with its fold and moat) and Clayton colliery are marked, but there is no Ashton New Road. Little Droylsden lies within Openshaw.

Introduction

Clayton and Openshaw in east Manchester both experienced rapid industrial growth which transformed their rural areas, followed by a slump and clearance schemes, which stripped their main roads of housing, shops and industry. Both townships, however, have played important and interesting parts in the history of Manchester.

Clayton lies north of Openshaw, with Clayton Brook dividing them. Together they form an 'upright coffin'-shaped area, stretching from Newton Heath and the River Medlock valley in the north down to Gorton and the Gorton/Corn Brook in the south. From the west they extend from Bradford and Ardwick, across eastwards to Edge Lane, Droylsden and Seventhorns Brook (late Fairfield Wells) at Audenshaw. The area of Fairfield stretches across the three townships of Droylsden, Audenshaw and Openshaw, which itself is divided into Higher Openshaw at its east end as far as Openshaw Canal Bridge, where it becomes Openshaw and then Lower Openshaw on its west side. Within Openshaw also once lay the triangular-shaped area of Little Droylsden (Abbey Hey), which was subsumed into Openshaw in 1889.

Clayton has been linked with Droylsden, since Clayton Hall was the centre of the sub-manor of Clayton with Droylsden within the manor of Manchester. Its name means 'settlement on clay' and its rural, wooded landscape provided clay, sandstone and coal. From medieval times the Clayton family lived at their hall, until the Byrons took possession for about thirteen generations. In around 1621 two merchant brothers, George and Humphrey Chetham, bought the estate; Humphrey was a great benefactor to Manchester. More recently the land passed to the Hoare family and the hall, still standing, to the city of Manchester. The manorial corn mill was at Mill House on the River Medlock, now called Clayton Bridge within the township of Newton Heath. In 1890 Clayton passed into the hands of the city of Manchester. Its population was only 1,600 in 1859 but grew rapidly in the nineteenth century, and then dropped as industry left the area.

The name Openshaw means 'unenclosed woodland'. Its population rose from around 117 in 1641 and 838 in 1831 to 2,280 in 1841 and 23,927 in 1891 through industrialisation. Openshaw was one of the townships within the manor and parish of Manchester, and so its mill was in the city centre. Until present times the Legh family of High Legh, Cheshire, has been the chief landowner since the early 1700s, when farming cleared away the woodland in both towns. Like Clayton, in 1890 Openshaw passed into the control of the city of Manchester.

The main roads developed horizontally across both towns. Ashton Old Road crosses Openshaw, and the turnpike road was opened in 1731 from Manchester to Saltersbrook, with toll gates near Grey Mare, Gorton and Ogden Lanes. In Clayton, Ashton New Road was built as a turnpike in 1826 and North Road was intended as a turnpike to Ashton by the owners of Clayton estates. Canals followed with the Manchester & Ashton Canal running south of and parallel to Ashton New Road from 1797, with a branch to Stockport from Clayton dividing Openshaw from Higher Openshaw, plus the shorter Clayton Arm. The railways followed, crossing north of Clayton across the Medlock viaduct and through the south part of Openshaw, with Ashbury's and Gorton and Openshaw stations, plus numerous junctions, sidings and locomotive works.

Clayton colliery produced coal which was transported along its own private road, Clayton Lane. The small village of Clayton was transformed into an industrial area of dyeworks, chemical plants, textile printworks and car production (Belsize Motors). Clayton Aniline has always been a large employer locally. The 'Clayton Smell' from these works, plus the bone yard and the colourful dyed faces of the workers, once epitomised Clayton.

Openshaw also grew dramatically as industry expanded. The noise of steam hammers and steam engines filled the air, which, like the brooks and rivers, was polluted. Farming, hatting, weaving and bleaching gave way to iron working, car production at Crossley Motors, locomotives at Gorton Tank, cranes at Vaughan's, tool-making at Joseph Whitworth's, suet refining at the Atora works, brewing and electrical engineering. Many of these works straddled the border with Gorton.

Housing sprang up everywhere, with rows of terraced houses for the workers and planned better-class homes for the managers and owners. North Road in Clayton and Fairfield in Higher Openshaw were the domain mainly of the better-class housing. The main roads were lined with houses, shops and numerous public houses. Thirty-five pubs lined Ashton Old Road alone, most of which are now gone.

Churches and schools followed, including three Anglican, one Moravian, numerous Methodist and three Roman Catholic churches. There were church schools, council board schools, Openshaw Technical College and Gorton Tank school for employees' children. Public buildings were few with no town halls, but Whitworth Hall, the public baths and library were built on Ashton Old Road in Openshaw. Next door stands Crossley Lads' Club. William and Frank Crossley were benevolent employers locally. Leisure was provided by public libraries, various parks and recreation grounds, theatres such as the Metropole and Alhambra in Openshaw and cinemas like the Carlton in Clayton and the Regal and Imperial in Openshaw. Maynes coaches in Clayton pioneered transport and leisure outings. Sports teams abounded; it is in Clayton that Manchester United has its roots.

The recession in industry devastated the two areas, 'described as part of "Vulcan's anvil" during the Industrial Revolution and now less than a shadow of [their] former self' (*Gorton & Openshaw Reporter*, 1970).

This book contains photographs portraying street scenes, rural views, places and buildings of interest and the people at leisure, at work and shopping and also at church and school. Most of the photographs are from the family albums of local people, who are proud of the towns where their families lived for generations, and of the community spirit that held them together. The book is nostalgic for those who remember the towns in their heyday, and an eye-opener for those who know only main roads cleared of buildings and the East Manchester regeneration programme.

one

Street Scenes

Looking north along North Road, Clayton, from Ashton New Road, in the early 1900s.
On the right lies the 'Red Rec', a triangle bounded by North and Ashton New Roads and
Clayton Street. This recreation ground was opened as an extension to Clayton Hall Park (see
page 27). On the left, where housing and shops (including Hugh Fay's grocery) lie in the
picture, now stands the health centre and the Wells 'Sure Start' Centre.

The north-west side of North Road, Clayton, with Clayton Street left (*c.* 1910). Joseph
Pickvance, paint merchant and decorator, lived on this corner, which was called Church
View. His house was a surgery by the 1960s. Much of the housing is now demolished but the
furthest tall gable is still home to the Granelli family, icecream makers. Opposite lies Clayton
Hall recreation ground, now a park.

The west side of North Road after 1910, when the priests of St Willibrord's Roman Catholic church had moved from Clayton House (see page 30) to this house on the left. Their mission school/chapel, which was south of the present church, lay a short walk across North Road on Stanton Street. These houses still stand opposite Viola Street on the corner of Dreyfus Avenue.

The north-east end of North Road, near its junction with Edge Lane, Droylsden, in 1906. This large house, once home to the Davies family, is now a residential home. The poster on the gatepost advertises a performance by Clayton Dramatic Society.

Ashton New Road in Clayton, with North Road leading off into the distance (*c.* 1960).
The trolley bus is on the corner of Croft Street. Left of the car is Robinson's furniture and
pawnshop and further up is the old Clayton library; to the right of centre is a police box.

The south side of Ashton New Road in Clayton, viewed from near its junction with North
Road in the early 1900s. The chimneys of Clayton Aniline dyeworks are in the distance. Off
to the left stands the Grove Inn.

The south side of Ashton New Road (with Turner Street off to the left), Clayton, in the early 1900s. On the corner stands the Green's Arms public house, with a datestone from 1837. The Empire grocery and provision store lies across Turner Street. A Co-operative store adjoins the public house. This was a branch of the Beswick Co-operative Society in 1878. By 1914 it belonged to the Droylsden Industrial Co-operative Society. It had a grocery, drapery, butchery and reading rooms. More recently it was Donahey's dance school.

The site of the future 'Openshaw village' (1978). This 'Site of the Year' was a council housing estate with roads named Aviemore, Stan Jolly and Tarland Walks and Kingcraig Close. Completed in 1980, it stood on the site of a former steel works, adjoining Clayton Aniline complex at its lower end and lying close to other industrial works.

Graham Street in December 1976. The street lay mostly within Openshaw but Nos 1 to 5 on the north side were in Bradford.

Graham Street as viewed from the site of the old cinema, which became the Domino club. Bosworth Street, also in Openshaw, lies on the right. This marked the western edge of Openshaw, where it adjoined Bradford.

Ashton Old Road in Openshaw, looking east, in 1919. Grey Mare Lane leads off left, where the original Grey Mare Tavern stands on the corner, and Pottery Lane turns off right opposite. A double-decker tram mingles with horses and carts. On the left by Thornton Street lies a branch of the Manchester and Salford Savings Bank, near to the Penny Bazaar. This major junction straddled the complex boundary between Openshaw, Bradford and Gorton.

Ashton Old Road looking west, 1940. Pottery Lane turns off on the left and Grey Mare Lane on the right, beyond the edge of the Grey Mare Hotel, with its old façade now covered in white tiles. Beyond the lane stands another white-tiled building, a furniture dealer's showroom. From the left lie the edge of the Hand & Heart public house, Longworth's Empire wine shop, an ironmongery, a tripe dresser, a confectioner and the Britannia Inn on the corner of Pottery Lane, with a branch of William and Deacon's bank on the opposite corner.

The north side of Ashton Old Road in Fairfield, Higher Openshaw (*c.* 1920). The tall façade of St Anne's Roman Catholic church looms behind the tram, which is passing the Grove Inn with Club Street on the near side. Housing and a shop lead along to the Crown Inn and the property named 'Seven Thorns'. Its nameplate and the building still exist. In 1878 it was home to a priest and to a private school.

Ashton Old Road looking eastwards in 1905. On the left the edge of the Grove Inn, a beer retailer until around 1914, adjoins the house at the entrance to elegant Gransmoor Avenue. Next to the matching house beyond the entrance are the Roman Catholic manse, church and school of St Anne's, with Fairfield Terrace in the distance. On the right side housing lines the road where Rose Bank House and the mission church and school of St Anne's stood nearby in 1878.

Opposite above: Ashton Old Road, Openshaw looking north, 1924. Sandywell Street leads off on the right, with Hardon's shop on its corner. Established in 1840, this double-fronted shop was a pawnbrokers, dealing in jewellery, furnishing and drapery. In 1914 James Watson Hardon was the pawnbroker, with the Droylsden Co-operative boot department next door, followed by a drapery and a greengrocery.

Opposite below: The north side of Ashton Old Road, Higher Openshaw leading right to Audenshaw (*c.* 1914). Housing adjoining Duffield's newsagents ends at Mersey Street. Next come John Clayton's ('fish and potato dealer & restaurant'), Thomas Turner's (a plumber), Archibald Proctor's greengrocery and Henry Heys' confectionery. Across Beck Street lies a branch of the Manchester & Liverpool Bank, Maund's (a tailors), Vernon's provisions shop and Sunderland's ironmongery.

Fairfield Terrace, Ashton Old Road (now demolished), Fairfield, Higher Openshaw, looking eastwards in the early 1900s. On the left is the edge of the site occupied by St Anne's Roman Catholic school, church and manse. In the distance lies the tall row of shops named Station View and opposite is the turning into Manshaw (late Station) Road, where once stood Auburn House.

Station View, looking west along Ashton Old Road in 1922. On the right lies Fairfield Road and the borders between Openshaw, Audenshaw and Droylsden, and also between the city of Manchester and Tameside MBC. Fairfield crosses three townships: Audenshaw, Droylsden and Openshaw. The right-hand shop is the tram office and the left-hand shop the post office. Fairfield View and the church site follow, lying opposite Fairfield Wells (see page 26).

two

Rural Scenes

Above: A drawing of the back of Clayton Hall in 1889. Behind the hall lie the church of St Cross and the chimneys of the dyeworks and other factories. The medieval moat, with its bridge, encloses the two-acre raised site, with the hall nestling in its south-east corner. Lying three miles east of Manchester, the area is now bounded by North Road, Ashton New Road and Clayton hall Road (late Park Street).

Left: The statue of Humphrey Chetham: merchant, money lender, government official and philanthropist (1580-1653) on Manchester Town Hall. The Clayton family sold the Clayton Hall estate to the Byrons in 1199. Thirteen generations later, in around 1621, through debt, they sold the manor of Clayton and Droylsden to brothers George and Humphrey Chetham for £4,700. Humphrey became High Sheriff of Lancashire. He endowed in his will the foundation of Chetham's school and public library.

The west back of Clayton Hall, with the church of St Cross (*c.* 1910). Originally set around a quadrangle or with three wings, the remaining original two-storey timber-framed house was extended by Humphrey Chetham in the seventeenth century. A north wing was added in the early eighteenth century and a corridor on the west side with a projecting staircase and gable.

The east front of Clayton Hall in 1906. In the north-west corner there was an oratory or chapel, licensed for services from around 1400. It was demolished in the early eighteenth century after being used as piggeries and even toilets. The old font went to Manchester Cathedral. The bell in its wooden tower, one of a set of four and said to originate from Manchester Cathedral, is inscribed *J'attende meleor* (or 'I await better things') and bears a rose and crown.

The bridge across the moat of Clayton Hall in 2004. Originally a drawbridge crossed this running stream. Foundations of earlier buildings were found in the moat, which is probably unique in Manchester. Later a narrow bridge was erected, which was widened in the nineteenth century to create this stone, two-arched bridge with a low parapet and tall iron entrance gates set between stone piers.

Fishing in Clayton Vale in the 1970s. Bill Jeffries fishes at a pond, watched by his dog Sammy. The vale lies on the banks of the River Medlock off Bank Street, and forms a border between Clayton, Newton Heath and Bradford. Recent regeneration has greatly improved Clayton Vale Park. One area, the Dingle, lay off Clayton and Vale Streets, and sports activities such as golf, football and cricket took place there.

Above: Green Fold in Higher Openshaw (1918). Nicknamed the 'Favourite Walk', Green Fold cuts between Gorton's lower and upper reservoirs through Debdale Vale. Following an Act of 1823, they were completed in 1826 by Manchester and Salford Waterworks and passed to Manchester Corporation in 1851. No longer needed as a water supply, since 1963 they have been used for leisure pursuits, bordering Debdale Park and two golf courses.

Opposite, below: Clayton Hall cottage, set back off Ashton New Road, near Clayton Conservative Club. Before Ashton New Road, an old lane ran from Clayton Hall across the moat to this four-acre fold, south-east of the hall. Here stood the wheat barn, later to become a farmhouse until its demolition. Here also were the great barn, steep-pitched and thatched, which burned down in 1852, and the oat barn, with six cruck frames, which was in existence until around 1877.

The locks on the Manchester & Ashton Canal at the bottom of Crabtree Lane, Clayton (2004). The canal was opened in 1797, with an extension to Stockport. Here there was a swivel bridge to give public access across the canal from Clayton through to Openshaw. This eventually reached Old Lane and Ashton Old Road, where Henry Crabtree had his dyeworks.

Fairfield Wells in Fairfeld, Higher Openshaw (1890). As they were drained in 1890, this drawing is all we have to depict how rural the border was between Audenshaw, Droylsden and Openshaw. Lying just south of Ashton Old Road, this source of water was the original water supply for the Moravian settlement. It was also known as 'Seventhorns' and later as 'St Anne's Wells', after the building nearby of St Anne's Mission church.

Clayton Hall Park in the early 1900s. Opened in 1893 on an eight-acre site between North Road and Ashton New Road, the park lies adjacent to Clayton Hall on its estate with an extension across Clayton Street. It had two bowling greens, a children's playground and this rest shelter. Also in Clayton, the Hewlett Johnston playing fields, between Seymour Road and Edge Lane, were opened after the Second World War, with a playground added in 1964.

Delamere Park, off Ashton Old Road in Higher Openshaw, in the early 1900s. Bounded by Delamere and Latham Streets, with an entrance off the main road, this park gained two bowling greens, a children's playground, five tennis courts, a rest shelter and flower beds. Opened in 1899 by Manchester Corporation, its 8.7 acres were originally called 'Burkitt's Meadow' and were owned by the Legh family.

Above: Janet Sheldon in the playground in Greenside (late George) Street recreation ground, Openshaw in 1965. Meech Street lies on the left and in the south-east corner is Elysian Street school. The park had two bowling greens, a rest shelter, playground and pavilion. Opened in 1891 by Manchester Corporation, its six-acre site is now called Openshaw Park.

Left: Janet Sheldon, with Kipps the dog, sitting on the grass in Greenside Street recreation ground in 1964. In the background is the water tower of English Steel. In the Openshaw area, Manchester Corporation also opened Lees Street recreation ground, with its war memorial; Whyatt Street recreation ground (in 1897); Lily Thomas gardens; and Legh recreation ground (in 1930), off Ogden Lane, with its football pitch.

three

People, Places and Transport

Above: Clayton House, home to the first priests of St Willibrord's Roman Catholic church from 1906. In front stands a figure who is probably Father Charles Hanrahan, the first priest. Eventually the first prefabricated school was built on the site, separate from the first mission school/chapel. The priests next lived in a large house on North Road, and then a presbytery was built next to the church in 1954. Clayton House lay near the Methodist chapel on North Road. The Hobsons lived there in the early 1900s.

Left: Wellington Villas, on the north side of Ashton Old Road in Fairfield, Higher Openshaw (2004). Here (until 1891) lived John Battersby, a brewer, and his wife Fanny (see page 56). In 1878 he lived at Egerton Bank across the road near Latham Street. By 1914 Thomas Battersby was living at Wellington Villas. Battersby Street was named after the family; it runs between Capital Road (late City Street) and Abbey Hey Lane (late Abbey Street). John served on the Openshaw Local Board and was a Conservative and Freemason, but failed to be elected for Openshaw ward on Manchester City Council.

Clayton Conservative Club, on the corner of Ashton New Road and Clayton Hall Road (late Park Street). The war memorial stands across Park Street within Clayton Hall Park. The club's foundation stone was laid by Dr Charles Dreyfus, a city councillor in Manchester, who helped to found the Jewish hospital and who was the founder in 1876 of Clayton Aniline dyeworks. Dreyfus Avenue, off North Road, is named after him.

Higher Openshaw Conservative Club, on the south side of Ashton Old Road (2004). The foundation stones of this large building, which stretches as far as Capital Road (late City Street), were laid in May 1892 by Ernest Hatch, Mrs John ?, Cllr James Robinson and Alderman Chesters Thompson.

Openshaw Liberal Club on Greenside (late George) Street, off Ashton Old Road (2002). South Street turns off to its right. Now demolished and built over, it was known as the Granville Social Club, or just 'the Granville', as its foundation stone read, 'This memorial tablet was laid by Earl Granville KG, Nov 3 1888'. Upstairs was a dance hall with a resident pianist and drummer.

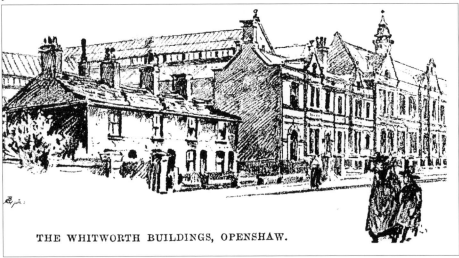

THE WHITWORTH BUILDINGS, OPENSHAW.

An 1889 drawing of the Whitworth buildings on Ashton Old Road, Lower Openshaw. This shows an adjoining row of old cottages long since demolished. On the left are the baths, dated 1890, and on the right is Whitworth Hall, dated 1894, with a public library behind. They were funded by Manchester City Corporation and by the legatees of Joseph Whitworth (see page 64). This public hall hosted many events, such as Crossley's penny concerts and even Keir Hardy's rally in 1910.

Above: The Whitworth buildings in 1905. The baths, designed by Beaumont, included public wash houses and a 'First Class' pool. By 1914 the library housed billiard and reading rooms, and the Openshaw Junior Technical School ran in its basement until 1931. During the war it housed service personnel and an air-raid shelter. The baths closed in 1969 but reopened in 1983 as the Whitworth centre for the disabled.

Right: Crossley House Youth Centre, adjoining the Whitworth buildings where the row of cottages had stood (2004). In 1896 William Crossley moved his Crossley Lads Club (founded 1888) from his works to the Mechanics' Institute on Pottery Lane, and then in 1913 to Crossley House. The building was designed for him by Broadbent, but used first in 1912 as a 'Home of Peace for Persons in Consumption', a hospital founded and maintained by the Crossley family. This club also housed the Openshaw Junior Technical School between 1914 and 1931, and eventually became a youth centre.

Left: Kurseong House at No. 1478 Ashton Old Road in Fairfield, Higher Openshaw (2004). On the south side of Ashton Old Road stand many elegant houses, such as Belvedere, Cavendish and Balgay (an area in Dundee in Scotland). Built in 1892, Kurseong was named after a district in Darjeeling in West Bengal, India. The name means 'the place of the white orchid'. In 1895 the Southerns lived there; in 1914, a timekeeper named Samuel Ford; and in 1965, Mr Alan Reddett.

Below: An open-topped double-deck horse-drawn Eades tram car on Ashton Old Road in Openshaw (*c.* 1902). Behind lies the north side of Ashton Old Road with Fairfield Road just off to the left, where the grocer's shop lies on its corner. By 1914 it had became Seymour Mead's grocery. Housing, destined to become a row of shops, lines the main road as far as the elegant, tall row of shops, ending at a bank and Beck Street.

Left: A line of special electric tram cars on North Road in Clayton, sometime after 1903. On the right is visible the church of St Cross on Ashton New Road. The occasion is for the Sons of Temperance (of Bradford) celebrating a 'Good Intent Show' for the 650 boys and girls who are crowding the trams.

Below: A horse-drawn single-deck Eades tram car on Ashton Old Road (*c.* 1902). Its destinations include Gorton Lane. The tram car depot of the Manchester Carriage & Tramways Co. lay down Louisa Street in Openshaw.

Gorton & Openshaw station (in Openshaw) opened in 1906. Access was from Lees Street and south of it, visible on the right, lies Varna Street school. This station was a replacement for Gorton station (off Cornwall Street), and originally it had corrugated iron and wooden buildings, which were later replaced.

Ashbury's station, Lower Openshaw, in the early 1900s. Lying west of Pottery Lane, it proudly proclaimed 'Ashbury's for Belle Vue'. Although giving easy access to this pleasure park, it was probably opened for the employees of Ashbury's Railway Carriage & Wagon works, north of the station. Opened in 1855 by the Great Central Railway Co. and located alongside the Gorton Brook pottery, its original buildings were demolished in the 1990s but the station is still in use.

Ashbury's station, Lower Openshaw, viewed from the opposite direction. It adjoined complex sidings called the Ashbury's Sidings, and further sidings ran into nearby works, including the Great Central Railway locomotive works, usually nicknamed 'Gorton Tank', (see pages 66-7). In 1875 another line was opened from Ashbury East Junction to Romiley Junction, via the newly opened Belle Vue Station, by the Sheffield & Midland Joint Railway Co.

Timothy and James Gregory play outside the Barrington Street pensioners' club in Clayton (1976). They lived next door to the club. In the background lies Barrington Street, with some of its two-up two-down housing. This street runs parallel to and north of North Road, eastwards from Clayton Street to Vale Street.

Left: Elizabeth Wells, aged 102 (2004). Elizabeth was born in Clayton in 1902. She attended Seymour Road school. She remembers skating on the frozen moat of Clayton Hall. At age thirty-three she married Bill, a galvaniser at Johnson's, but Elizabeth did not work after their marriage. In 1937 they had a daughter, Elizabeth Marshall. In 2001 she opened her namesake, the Wells 'Sure Start' Centre, opposite Clayton Library, where she attends a local history group.

Below: Members of the local history group at Clayton Library working with pupils from Seymour Road Primary School in 2004. Together they helped to produce the 'East Manchester Works' exhibition for the new community gallery at the Museum of Science and Industry. The group has also produced a book of their memories. Anti-clockwise from Elizabeth Wells are members May Davies and Maggie Reed.

Brothers Steven and Anthony McNicholls on their back doorstep in Barrington Street, Clayton, 1971.

Maggie Richardson (*née* Hollingsworth) on the left with her friend Mrs Stean in the 1920s. Maggie's daughter is Maggie Reed. They are standing in the back entry of Maggie's home on Hackle Street, Clayton. North Road in the background runs parallel with Hackle Street, ending at Bagot Street.

Above, left: Jacqueline Oliver (*née* Payton) with Esther the cat, standing on Hackle Street, Clayton in the 1950s. She is the daughter of Lillian Payton.

Above, right: Lillian Payton, mother of Jacqueline, standing on Stanton Street, Clayton in the late 1920s. Behind her is where the Eastern by-pass would later be built, running to Schofield Street. The mission church of St Willibrord stood on Stanton Street on the corner of Bagot Street.

Left: Terry Potter, nephew of Bill and Joan Jeffries (see page 89), in the 1970s. He lived next to the shops behind him on Folkestone Road East in Clayton. These are now demolished. This large estate, built by the 1930s, lies north of North Road.

Above: An outing in the early 1900s. Elizabeth Walton (*née* Oliver), sits directly behind the driver. Her father George Oliver was a master builder, said to have built Oliver and Gresham Streets in Lower Openshaw, which lay just on the town's west border with Ardwick. Both ran from Ashton Old Road to Manipur and Church Streets respectively in Bradford. Oliver Street had its own war memorial for that area.

Right: Jerome Caminada (1844–1914), a detective chief inspector with Manchester police. Of Irish-Italian parentage, he joined up in 1868 and retired as a superintendent. He wrote about his famous detective work in *Twenty-Five Years of Detective Life* in 1895. From 1907 until 1910 he was an independent representative for Openshaw Ward on Manchester City Council.

Left: Marlene Sheldon, standing on Connie Street in Openshaw (1966). The works of English Steel lie in the background. These buildings have long since gone and Connie Street is now open at the end with roads through to Clayton. It lies north of Greenside Street recreation ground and runs south to Meech Street.

Below, left: Maria Sykes (aged eighty-one) cleaning her doorstep in 1967. Her home for sixty-four years was Kendall Street in Openshaw, until she was 'requested to leave' for house clearance. Kendall Street ran south from Wilson Street to George Street, east of Grey Mare Lane.

Below, right: Sisters Janet and Marlene Sheldon cuddling their new puppy Kipps in 1964. They are on Connie Street in Openshaw, standing by a Ford Zodiac car.

Children playing in Rushton Grove day nursery off Lees Street, Openshaw, in the early 1970s. Behind them lies the 'Red Rec', officially named Lees Street recreation ground, and beyond that Hugon's works (see pages 56-8). The railway line and Gorton & Openshaw station are nearby (see page 36).

Dawn Bullock (left) and Michelle Thompson on Boscastle Street, Openshaw, during the summer of 1972. Louisa Street used to cross Boscastle Street behind them, where demolition is taking place. In the distance is Old Lane. Boscastle Street lay near the canal, north of Ashton Old Road.

Above: Bobby Easthope and Dave Lockwood outside Bobby's home on Connie Street, Openshaw in 1965. They played the northern cabaret clubs as 'Bob and Dave' in the 1960s. In the background are the works of English Steel.

Left: Janet Sheldon, aged fifteen, playing the 'backyard blues' in the backyard at home in Connie Street, Openshaw (*c.* 1968). Connie Street is north of Greenside Street recreation ground.

four

Shopping
and Work

The main offices of the Beswick Co-operative Society on Grey Mare Lane in Openshaw (1959). Established on 4 June 1892, this society later built these offices between Whyatt and Bosworth Streets, near Openshaw's boundary with Bradford. It housed the society's offices, including departments such as Grocery, and had a laundry on the corner of Whyatt Street. It was demolished to make way for road improvements.

Branch No. 8 of the Beswick Co-operative Society at 37 Ashton Old Road, Lower Openshaw, in the early 1900s. Standing near the town's border with Ardwick, in 1878 it had been the Openshaw Loan Society. It opened as a grocery shop on 24 May 1900. The neighbouring Manchester & Salford Co-operative Society lodged a complaint as they had hoped to take it over, and co-operative societies formed boundary agreements. By 1914 the shop had become a branch of the Lancashire Hygienic Dairies.

Branch No. 11 of the Beswick Co-operative Society, between Vincent and Croft Streets in Openshaw, in its early days .This grocery shop opened in December 1905 after a procession from the Rowsley Street main branch, accompanied by a brass band. Initially there were about eighty members and membership cost 6d. By 1907 a butchers shop was added. The original shop was built by Messrs Wooller & Sons of Eccles and cost £938, plus £1,200 for fittings.

The main Openshaw branch of the Droylsden Industrial Co-operative Society on the south side of Ashton Old Road in Higher Openshaw (2004). Bounded by Swindells, Stanley and Vine Streets, the empty building still dominates the shopping area. Initiated by the Dukinfield Co-operative Society, this independent society was set up in 1861, opening here *c.* 1900. Its beehive symbol tops the front façade, designed by Edwin Marshall, but its twin minarets have gone. Upstairs was a hall used for functions and dancing and accessed at the back.

No. 10 branch of the Droylsden Industrial Co-operative Society on the corner of Stockholm and Ravensbury Streets in Clayton (2002). Standing near Ravensbury school and erected in 1908, it carries the symbolic badge of the society, plus a coronet-capped tower. Other small branches existed in Clayton and Openshaw. The Newton Heath Co-operative Society had one branch on Lees Street in Openshaw in 1850. The Manchester & Salford Co-operative Society also had branches in Openshaw.

A plaque marking the location of Clayton market place on Ashton New Road, near the turning for North Road. Fairfield market place has a similar plaque above a shop on Ashton Old Road near Delamere Street. Small markets in Openshaw existed between Odgen Lane and Vine Street, and between Wellington and Barmouth Streets. Smithfield fruit and vegetable market moved from Manchester city centre to Openshaw's forty-seven acres off Ogden Lane in 1974.

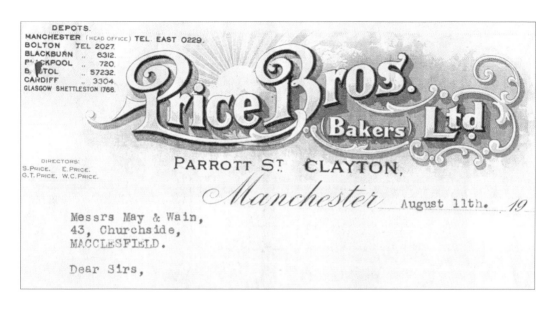

A billhead for Price Brothers bakers, of Parrott Street in Clayton (1943). In 1878 Price Brothers also had branches on Ashton Old Road: on the north side at No. 1245 and on the south side at No. 326. They had many depots across the country, but Parrott Street was their head office.

Ashton House, W. Lomas' pork butchery and grocery shop at 126 Ashton Old Road, Lower Openshaw (1892). Godrey Bintcliffe opened this business in 1871 and was renowned for his pork products. After Mr Bintcliffe's death in 1886, Mr Lomas took over and expanded the business between Edmund (on the right) and Ashbury Streets, on the south side of Ashton Old Road. Included were slaughterhouses and pork curing, sausage-making and pie-making rooms, all driven by steam power.

Postal Address:—401, Grey Mare Lane, BRADFORD.   Telephone No. 663, Openshaw

Residence:—1, Harrop Street, Abbey Hey Lane, GORTON.

SALE YARD AND MORTAR MILL:—Adjoining GREY MARE HOTEL,

Openshaw, *31 Oct* 191*1*

M. Harrop & Brown Chgl *Edge Lane Contract.*

To JOHN OWEN & SONS, Dr.,

BUILDERS AND CONTRACTORS.   PUBLIC MORTAR MILL

(Order No 1183)

Oct To Mill at Edge Lane 1 Ton 1 cwt of Mort

A billhead for John Owen & Sons, who were located off Ashton Old Road, Openshaw in 1911. This firm of builders and contractors had their sale yard and public mortar mill adjacent to the Grey Mare Hotel, on the east side of Grey Mare Lane, between Oxford and Dunkirk Streets. In 1966 the firm acquired more premises on Chapman Street in Gorton, when they took over Fishwick's at Openshaw.

The large flat-roofed store of Montague Burton, tailor and men's outfitter, on the corner of Ashton Old Road and Grey Mare Lane in Openshaw (1992). Ashton Old Road runs across the picture and Pottery Lane turns off bottom left. Burton's store, which adjoined the Manchester & Salford Bank and was designed in the 1930s by N. Martin, used its upper floor as a billiard hall. Originally small shops occupied this site, and then Clydesdale house furnishers. All this was eventually demolished for road improvements.

Edward Pemberton's cycle store at 289-291 Ashton Old Road in Openshaw, in the early 1900s. He opened as a cycle-maker in 1896. His three sons pose with his cycles: Fred (born 1899), Albert and Bernard. In *c.* 1911 the business moved to Stockport Road in Longsight. The firm produced the famous 'Pemberton Arrow' cycles and tandems, as well as crystal wireless sets. Famous cyclists rode these hand-made cycles, for example in the 1934 British Empire Games, where Fred officiated.

A row of shops on Ashton Old Road, Openshaw in the early 1960s. Off to the left is Kirkham Street, with Valentine's self-service store, advertising as bacon specialists. Next comes Westwell's drapery, then Thomas' greengrocery and finally F. Allen's hairdressers shop, which became Harwood's in 1965. Off to the right lay the Fountain Inn, next to Turton Street.

Left: Stanley Hodson's gentlemen's outfitters shop at No. 809 Ashton Old Road, Openshaw in the 1950s. This row of shops ended at Wood Street, where the Lord Wolseley public house stood on the opposite corner (see page 92). On the corner is Stanyer's butchers shop, which had been a greengrocery in 1878, when Hodson's was a pawnbrokers. Next door is a hairdressers, and off the photograph is a newsagents. Off to the left lies Whitworth Hall.

Below: A Whit Walk procession in the late 1950s, with (a rather surprised-looking) Marjorie Bullock in front. Behind them on the south side of Ashton Old Road lies a Timpson's shoe shop, on the corner of Dereham (late Hope) Street. A beer retailer is on the opposite corner, next to Davies' ladies clothes shop, which by 1965 was a confectioners.

An advertisement for Timpson's shoe shops on Ashton Old Road in Openshaw (1948).

A COMPLETE FOOTWEAR SERVICE

● SHOES ● HOSIERY
● HANDBAGS ● REPAIRS

TIMPSON
Shoe Shops

531 & 1194 ASHTON OLD ROAD
312/4 ASHTON NEW ROAD
AND THROUGHOUT MANCHESTER AND DISTRICT

Shops on the south side of Ashton Old Road, Higher Openshaw in the early 1900s. At No. 648 (later 1206), a sign in Thomas Hodson's grocery boasts, 'This is the Irish bacon shop'. His business was there in 1905, with another shop at 437 Ashton Old Road by 1914. Next door at No. 646 is 'The People's Butcher', where M. Ewen ran his business in 1914. Both shops became the Star cycle shop by 1965. On the left is Greenall's herbalist shop, near the corner of Andrew Street.

Above: Atkinson's Dairy on Bowness Street, off Ashton Old Road in Higher Openshaw, in the early 1900s. The horse and cart belong to the dairy and bear the sign 'W. Atkinson' on the front of the cart. The house, where the woman and child stand, has 'Atkinson's Dairy' on the glass panel over the front door and a card declaring 'Pure New Milk' in the front window.

Left: A shop on the corner of Fairfield Road and Toxteth Street, Higher Openshaw (*c.* 1924). Ethel, Harold and Lily Butler stand outside as they prepare for a Whit Walk procession. The shop stood near the Salvation Army citadel. An amazing array of brushes and goods is set out in the window. A notice reads, 'The household sweeping brush'. Tins of Duradio paint stand above Vesta quick-drying paintbrushes.

The building now known as Elizabeth House, formerly the Empire Model Laundry, at No. 1554 Ashton Old Road, Fairfield, Higher Openshaw in 1960. Its lofty curved façade is topped with urns, inset with carvings and inscribed in stone. It adjoined a row of terraced cottages on the left and had tall garage doors on the right. Known locally as 'The Empire', it was a communal wash house. In 1906 the proprietor was Mrs Jane Willoughby.

Window of the Cottage Inn on Hyde Road, Denton, etched with the brewery name Openshaw Ales. In 1860 William Wagster opened on Tamworth Street as the Openshaw Bridge brewery. In 1883 it was a company with £5,000 capital. The Pollitt family, of the Church Hotel on Ashton Old Road (see page 91), was involved from its early days, James Pollitt being the manager in 1888. Eventually the business moved to the Victoria brewery in West Gorton, becoming known as Openshaw brewery. It was demolished in 1964.

Left: John Battersby, owner of the Wellington brewery on Wellington Street, Lower Openshaw, which opened in around 1867. In 1888 he sold the brewery to Chesters, who leased it to John Henry Lees, and John Battersby became a director of Chesters. In 1895 John Henry Lees went to the Albert brewery and the Wellington was let to the Manchester Malt Vinegar Co. until it ceased operating in 1899. The main site was demolished in 1920.

Below: A billhead of Hugon & Co. from 1917. Their site on Ogden Lane in Higher Openshaw was originally occupied by the High Bank Mill, which was a cotton mill built in 1861 by George Henry Grimshaw. He named it after his home on High Bank, Gorton, just across the town's border. The mill closed down around the end of the First World War and the site was sold to Hugon & Co.

TE COUNCILLOR BATTERSB*
Photograph taken at Blackpool.

Telegraphic Address: "HUGON, MANCHESTER"   Telephone: **384 & 385** OPENSHAW.

HUGON & COMPANY L?

Offices & Works, OGDEN LANE. OPENSHAW.

M Commercial Stores Co. Ltd.,
BRINKLEY,
Cambs.

MANCHESTER,

August 10th. 1917. 191

Atora Works.

15 PRIZE MEDALS AWARDED

MANUFACTURERS OF
" **ATORA** "
Refined Beef Suet.

SOUP SQUARES & POWDER.

SAUCE POWDER

BARLEY LEMONADE POWDER

Contractors to the Admiralty.

SUPPLIED TO THE ARMY &
ALL THE POLAR EXPEDITIONS.

RECEIPTS ON OUR PRINTED FORMS ONLY
CAN BE RECOGNISED.

Trade Mark.

ESTABLISHED 1895.

TERMS:—NETT MONTHLY.

THIS INVOICE IS DUE AND
PAYABLE AT OPENSHAW.

The works of Hugon & Co. in 1986. The company, established in 1893, moved from Pendleton to High Bank Mill on Ogden Lane in around 1920. They converted the mill to produce their beef suet products and to refine lard. The Atora works were later extended and were bounded by Ogden Lane on the north side, the canal on the west and Varna Street on the east.

The last staff dinner dance of Hugon & Co., 1974. This was held at the Piccadilly Plaza Hotel just before the company closed in Openshaw and moved to Hartlepool. Here, from left to right, stand Jean and David Dore and Brian and Hilda Dewhurst.

Visit of retired staff together with serving staff in the yard at Hugon's, July 1962. Mrs Mary Adshead, forelady for many years, stands just right of the bull's horns. The Atora product made Hugon & Co. famous and gave the mill its name. The company made the housewife's job easier with this ready-shredded and ready-prepared beef suet. They had won fifteen prize medals by 1917, and on their billheads they proudly declared that they supplied the Admiralty, Army and polar expeditions.

Opposite, above: A billhead from the Openshaw Bridge ironworks on Tamworth Street in 1900. The firm of John Smith & Sons (established in Bennett Street, Ardwick, in 1860) moved to Higher Openshaw off Ashton Old Road, producing fire grates. John was a member of the Openshaw Local Board. In 1888 his sons, Fred and Samuel, took over. The works consisted of five showrooms, a foundry, enamelling works and workshops, and employed about 200 people by 1892. It closed in around 1937.

Opposite, below: Drawing of a machine invented by Joseph Stubbs, iron founder of Louisa Street, Openshaw in 1890. Started in Store Street in Manchester by his uncle Joseph Hetherington, the business, now at Mill Street in Ancoats, passed to Joseph Stubbs in 1870. The firm branched out to Openshaw in the 1890s. They were 'patentees of special machinery for winding, clearing and warping yarn' in the cotton mills. As the need for cotton declined, the Louisa Street site was closed down in 1966.

Near Manchester, *Novr* 29 *IB* 1900

Messr Mellor & Co *Rainow*

To John Smith & Sons, Dr.

Iron Founders.

TERMS
Monthly

P.O. Orders to
be made payable at
Higher Openshaw

Manufacturers of Kitchen ranges, Palisadings,

AND RAIN WATER GOODS OF ALL DESCRIPTIONS &c. &c.

	Cwt.	Qrs.	lbs.	Price.	£	s.	d.
1 Dble boiler Lft for 1574 front					£ 1	0	0

per T McKay Co. Crawford

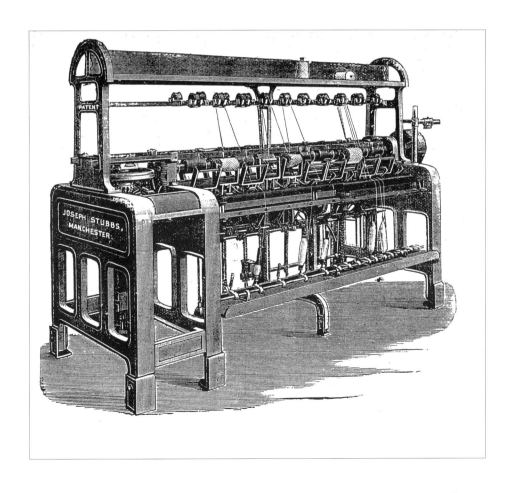

JOSEPH STUBBS,
MANCHESTER.

PATENT

Members of Cornwall Street Baptist church walk across Openshaw bridge, past the works of B. & S. Massey, in the early 1960s. The Openshaw Canal Bridge works, producing steam and power hammers, was founded in Higher Openshaw in 1861 by engineers Benjamin and Stephen Massey, on land north-east of the canal.

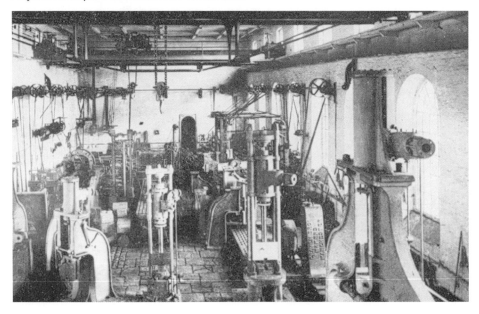

Interior of Massey's Openshaw ironworks, 1870. Originally intending to produce steam engines for the cotton mills, the brothers diversified their business during the cotton slump. The firm passed out of family control in 1971, merged in 1981 and was closed, with the works partially demolished, by 1984.

WADDING AND JEWELLERS' COTTON MANUFACTURERS AND DEALERS.

IMPERIAL (THE) PATENT WADDING CO. LIMITED

(manufacturers of cotton and man-made fibre wadding, cotton wool, absorbent wool, cotton felt and upholstery fillings);

Right: Trademark of the Imperial Patent Wadding Co. Ltd, sited at the Empire works on Turner Street, off Ashton Old Road in Clayton (1953). They manufactured cotton and man–made fibre wadding, cotton wool and cotton felt. The main office lay in Manchester on Tariff Street. In 1965 they became part of William Flanagan & Son.

Below: Billhead of the London Oil Refining Co., at the Lorco works off Croft Street in Clayton (1927). Established in 1890, the firm lay near Cantrell (late Chapel) and Aintree Streets in an area of dyeworks.

T.S. Dept. No. A. 154

PRIVATE BRANCH EXCHANGE.

ESTABLISHED 1890.

TELEPHONES:
OPENSHAW { 283
284

TELEGRAPHIC ADDRESS:
"PREMIER," MANCHESTER.

"LORCO" WORKS,

CLAYTON, Manchester, 26th January 19 27

Messrs The Bramall Park Golf Club Ltd.,   DATE DUE 25th February

Cheadle Hulme,

CHESHIRE.

To THE LONDON OIL REFINING CO. Dr.

PRINCIPAL: FRANK ANDREW.

OIL MANUFACTURERS AND REFINERS
OF HIGH GRADE TOILET OILS.

ORDER NO. 542

TERMS Nett % 30 Days

	Tons	Cwts.	Qrs.	Lbs.		Glns.	PRICE	£	s.	d.
1 x 5 gln Drum Antiseptic Liquid Soap.......@ 6/0d.								£ 1	10	0
							per gl.			

A Whit Walk procession passing the old tram depot on the north side of Ashton Old Road, on the corner of Louisa Street, Openshaw, in the early 1960s. In the distance is the Pack Horse public house. Hampson, Wrigley & Co., cotton raisers, operated here from 1877 until the 1960s, together with Benjamin Crompton, calico printers. Here also were S. Wacks & Co. (button manufacturers), Lindsay & Williams Ltd (cable-makers suppliers from the 1920s), Megotapes Ltd and Megotools Ltd.

Billhead of the Gorton Rubber Co. of Cornwall Street, Openshaw, from 1912. The works were on the east side of the road just off Ashton Old Road, north of Dewey Street. Another branch was in Droylsden at Edge Lane on the border with Openshaw.

Above: Letterhead of the firm Cooke & Ferguson Ltd, electrical welders and engineers of Victoria Street, Openshaw (1948). Located just off Ashton Old Road, the firm lay on the corner of South Street. By 1965 they produced electrical switchgear.

Right: General view, looking north-east, of the interior of the works of Ferguson, Pailin Ltd, Higher Openshaw (1932). Samuel Ferguson and George Pailin established their firm of electrical engineers in around 1913. They produced electrical switchgear. In 1925 they expanded into Buckley Street. In its early days the firm supplied local electricity and power plants for Stalybridge, Manchester Corporation and North Wales.

Top: Letterhead of the firm of Ferguson, Pailin Ltd from 1947. In around 1960 the firm merged with AEI, becoming part of GEC after another merger in 1968 and then ALSTOM in 1998. Expansion of the firm included a woodworking shop, boilerhouse, bar stores and pump house. Staff welfare was important, including a sports ground, canteen, social club, library and even an ambulance. In 1939 the firm purchased Mottram Hall, with its 130 acres, as a holiday home for their employees.

Above: Plaque to Sir Joseph Whitworth (1803-1887), erected in 1974 at Openshaw Technical College, which was built on his works site. He invented a standardised screw thread called the 'Whitworth Thread' and pioneered machine-made tools. Concerned for his workforce's education, he donated money for the Whitworth Scholarship scheme. In his will he provided for the foundation of Whitworth Hall on Ashton Old Road (see pages 32-3) and the Whitworth art gallery on Oxford Road.

Manchester, his engineering firm moved to Whitworth Street in Openshaw in 1880, employing around 780 people. In 1897 it merged to become Armstrong, Whitworth & Co. Producing armaments during the First World War and later relying on machine tools, the firm merged again in the 1920s to become Vickers Armstrong.

The office staff, including James Sheldon (far left), outside the works of English Steel in 1949. Created by another merger in 1929, they concentrated on the small tool and steel tool business at the North Street works of Armstrong, Whitworth in Openshaw. Vickers Armstrong produced armaments such as the Bofors gun during the Second World War, but closed in around 1950. In the early 1970s, Edgar Allen (steels) and Edgar Allen (tools) took over the North Street works of English Steel. They closed down in 1980.

Above: The interior of the Gorton Locomotive works, known as Gorton Tank. This carriage and wagon works of the Great Central Railway Co. (originally the Manchester, Sheffield & Lincoln Co.) straddled the border of Gorton and Openshaw, lying between Bessemer and Cornwall Streets in Openshaw. Designed by Richard Peacock and completed in 1848, it produced and repaired steam locomotives, exporting worldwide.

Left: On the right stands Jim Vardy, foreman coppersmith at Gorton Tank, in the early 1950s. The name Gorton Tank may have originated from the use of filtered canal water, pumped from the nearby canal and stored in a 30,000-gallon tank on Cornwall Street.

The interior of the brass finishing shop off Press (late Princess) Street at Gorton Tank in the 1950s. The site was vast and complex and included the 'Birdcage Walk', which was a wire mesh-enclosed walkway, running at roof-top level and linking Widnes (late Wellington) Street in Openshaw with Railway Street in Gorton.

The stores staff standing outside their offices in Gorton Tank in 1960. Second from the left stands Dorothy Lord (*née* Vardy). The 'Beeching Axe', whereby the minister Beeching closed many railway stations, forced the works to close in 1963, putting 1,700 people out of work. The forty-seven-acre site became home to Manchester's Smithfield wholesale fruit and vegetable market.

The works identity card of Edward McGuirk (1940). He worked for the firm of Laurence, Scott & Electromotors of Higher Openshaw. Both firms operated from Louisa Street, off Ashton Old Road. Electromotors engineering was there in 1914 and amalgamated with Laurence, Scott engineering between the two world wars. The 650-strong workforce was reduced to ten by 1981, when most of the work was transferred to Norwich and the machinery was airlifted out of the factory.

Francis Crossley (1839-1897), businessman and philanthropist. Together with his brother William, Frank founded Crossley Engines and Crossley Motors. As a Christian he provided spiritual and moral welfare and social amenities for his workmen. Frank supported financially and personally the local Salvation Army, the Manchester City Mission and the Star Mission Hall at Ancoats. Francis Crossley established his firm in Manchester in 1866 and with his brother William moved to new works on Pottery Lane, Openshaw in 1882. They became the patent holders of the Otto gas engines; the works straddling the Gorton/Openshaw border were named the Otto gas engine works.

A Crossley town gas slide engine, built in 1882 and working until 1929 in a London warehouse. By 1906 they were also producing cars at their Openshaw works. In 1910 they added two tall erecting shops nearby for car and bus production on Gorton Lane. Crossley Motors produced hand-built, large, expensive cars.

CONTRACTORS TO H. M. ADMIRALTY, WAR OFFICE, AIR MINISTRY AND DOMINION GOVERNMENTS.

TELEGRAMS: 'GASENGINE, MANCHESTER.'
TELEPHONE: (MANCHESTER) EAST 1353.

SPECIALISTS IN DIESEL ENGINES
GAS ENGINES·GAS PRODUCER PLANTS

CROSSLEY BROTHERS LTD.

Established 1867

WORKS ALSO AT STOCKPORT & NOTTINGHAM
LONDON OFFICE:

OPENSHAW
MANCHESTER · II

LANGHAM HOUSE,
308, REGENT ST., W.1.

OUR REF. HS/KA

YOUR REF.

Date 13th Jan. 1948.

Letterhead of Crossley Brothers Ltd, Openshaw, 1948.

Crossley–Premier Engines

P.O. Box 1, Manchester M11 2DP, England

Telephones: 223 1353 (STD Code 061)   Telex: 668975
Telegrams and Cables: Crossley, Manchester

DIESEL ENGINES · S.E.M.T.-PIELSTICK LICENSEES

Letterhead of Crossley-Premier Engines Ltd, Openshaw 1968. In 1927 ten 1926-model Crossley cars were used in Australia for the visit of the Duke of York (the future George VI), giving royal approval to the firm. By 1928 Crossleys were also producing medium-priced family cars in single-storey workshops on Crossley Street in Gorton.

The works of Crossley Engines in 1991. By 1951 Crossley Motors had moved out to their Crossley Road works in Heaton Chapel, where they had produced aeroplanes during the First World War. Since 1966 mergers and takeovers have seen the Crossley engine powering ships and generating electricity installations worldwide. In 1989 Rolls-Royce took over Crossley Engines, and since 1998 the name Crossley has been dropped.

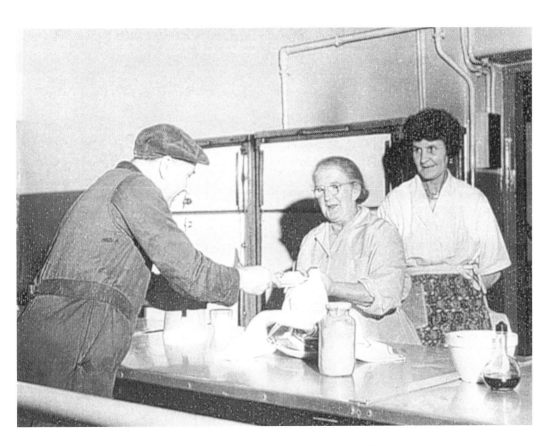

The canteen of Crossley Motors on Pottery Lane (*c.* 1957). Mary Prescott serves up a meal to one of the workers. Within their works the Crossley brothers had a chapel with a minister for their workforce. They were deeply religious, cared for their workers' welfare and promoted temperance. No Crossley gas engines went to breweries in the early years. They started the Crossley Lads' Club in a room in the works.

Trademark of the East Lancashire Chemical Co., which was based at Fairfield Road in Fairfield in 1892. Their site straddled across Higher Openshaw and Droylsden. Founded in 1840, they produced chemicals for the nearby textile trade, including pure soda crystals and various dyes.

Advertisement for the East Lancashire Chemical Co. (1966). The site was conveniently near the Manchester Canal, as well as the Lancashire & Yorkshire railway. In 1892 a new works was built with mechanics shops, a cooperage and smithy. They also had a city office on Market Street in Manchester.

Above: The new works of the East Lancashire Chemical Co. (bearing the inscription 'ELC Co. 1892') on Edge Lane in Fairfield, seen here in 1998. They also added workers' homes on Edge Lane in 1895, calling them 'East Lancashire Cottages'.

Opposite, below: Billhead showing a drawing of the works of the Clayton Aniline Co. in the 1910s. Founded by Charles Dreyfus in 1876, the works stood by the Ashton Canal for transport and for a water supply. Over the years the works were extended to over fifty-seven acres, and exported worldwide. Dreyfus was a pioneer in aniline dyes, producing dyes for cotton and wool and later synthetic materials for the nearby textile trade. They were the largest home producers of aniline oil and aniline salt.

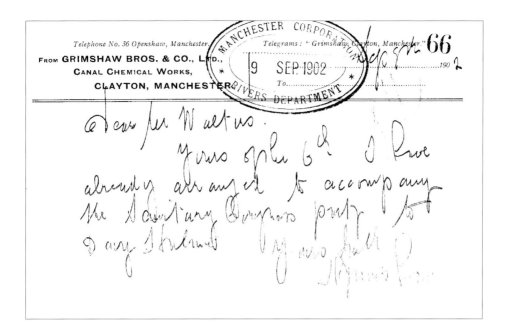

Postcard for Grimshaw Brothers & Co. of the Canal Chemical works in Clayton (1902). It concerns work they were to carry out for Manchester Corporation. In 1900 the firm was near the canal on Chatham Street, off Ashton New Road. They were also dry salters.

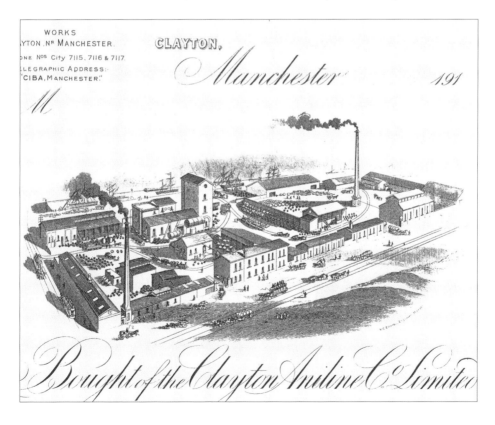

Above: A later letterhead of the same company, from 1946.

Left: Two trademarks of Clayton Aniline Co. The earlier one was registered in 1888, and later the horse's head was remodelled and the monogram CAC was added. It is unclear why they chose a horse's head. Their motto was *Arte et Industria*, Latin for 'With skill and hard work'.

Advertisement for the Clayton Aniline Co. from 1948. It shows an outline of the works and the motto 'The symbol of Service in the World of Dyestuffs'. In 1911 the company became CIBA's first United Kingdom site. During both world wars they produced explosives. They provided a convalescence home in Wales for their workers, which later became a holiday home.

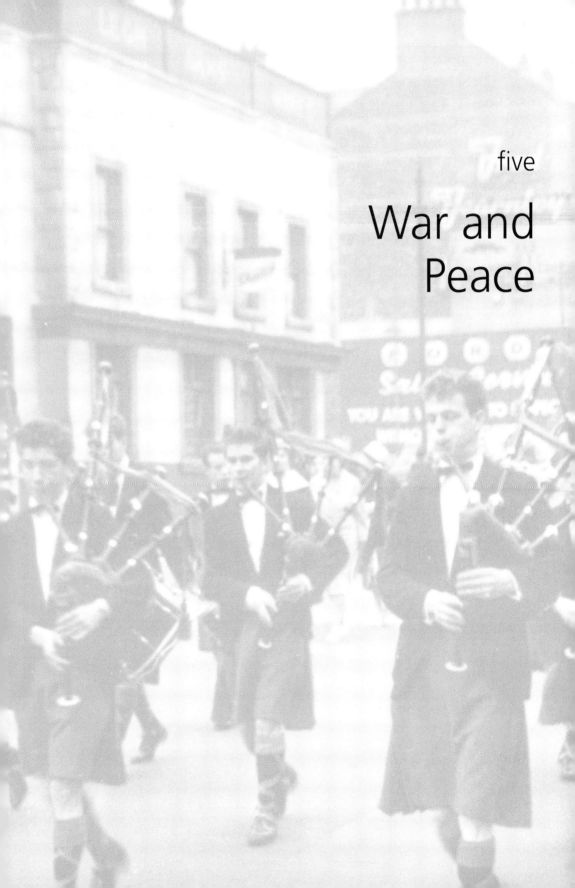

five

War and
Peace

Above: The gravestone of John Redditt VC (1897-1964) of Clayton. Born in Bamford Street, he attended St Cross church day school and played football in the Manchester Sunday school league. He joined his father as a clogger and shoe repairer on Ashton New Road, repairing boots for Manchester United Football Club. Serving in the South Lancashire Regiment in Mesopotamia, in 1917 John won the Victoria Cross for his bravery against enemy machine-gun fire. He returned to the cobblers shop, lived at Clayton Bridge and is buried in Gorton cemetery.

Above, right: John Richardson with his fiancée Florrie Wilson, both of Clayton, at Blackpool (*c.* 1939). John lived at Hackle Street and served in the Army during the Second World War. Florrie lived in Canberra Street.

Right: John and Florrie Richardson on their wedding day in June. Florrie was a Roman Catholic and John an Anglican, and so they got married in a Blackpool registry office. John's brother George and his wife attended as witnesses.

Left: The war memorial (remembering both world wars) on the corner of Lees Street and Abbey Hey Lane in Openshaw. Behind lies a caravan works. Small war memorials are found in schools, works and streets, such as the 'Oliver Street and District Roll of Honour' in Lower Openshaw for the First World War. The Grove Inn public house on Ashton New Road in Clayton placed a memorial in its vault to those killed during the First World War.

Below left: One side of the war memorial (dedicated to victims of both world wars) which stands in Clayton Hall Park on the corner of Ashton New Road and Clayton Park Road (late Park Street) in Clayton. Opposite it lies Clayton Conservative Club (see page 31), which conducted an annual remembrance service. Unveiled in 1921, the memorial holds 245 names; fifteen are for the Second World War, one for 'other conflicts' and 229 for the First World War.

Below: Part of the Roll of Honour from Belsize Motors Ltd of Clayton commemorating fifteen men from the office and 146 from the works. Their showroom was on Wilson Street, the works off Clayton Lane on Cycle Street and the garage near the canal bridge on Ashton Old Road. Marshall & Co. produced cars in the 1890s and then from 1900 to 1925 as Marshall & Belsize.

ROLL OF HONOUR.

BELSIZE MOTORS LTD.

Clayton, Manchester.

OFFICE.

CROWDER, S., *Royal Army Medical Corps.*
DUDLEY, Sergt. A., *Army Service Corps (M.T.).*
EARLE, A., *Army Service Corps.*
FLEMING, T., *Army Pay Corps.*
FOXLEY, J., *Army Service Corps.*
HALPIN, Corporal C., *Rifle Brigade*
HAMBLIN, G., *6th Batt. Manch/r Regt. (T.F.).*
HARTY, W., *Royal Engineers.*

HAYNES, Bomb. E., *Cnty. Palatine Artillery*
HIRST, E., *8th Batt. Manchester Regt. (T.F.)*
LYNCH, A., *8th Batt. Manchester Regt. (T.F.)*
MOLLARD, F., *4th Batt. Manchester Regt*
SMITH, Sergt.-Major J. A., *W. Yorkshire Regt*
TWISS, G., *Army Service Corps (M.T.).*
WHITNEY, R. J., *King's Liverpool Regt.*

WORKS.

ALDRED, R., *Rifle Brigade.*
ALLAN, W., *Army Service Corps.*
ASHTON, T., *9th Batt. Border Regt.*
ASHTON, F., *Royal Flying Corps.*
BARRACLOUGH, A., *Royal Engineers.*
BARTON, —, *6th Batt. Rifle Brigade.*
BAYBUT, H., *19th Batt. Manchester Regt*
BAYLE, M., *8th Batt. Manchester Regt. (T.F.)*
BELLAMY, B., *Royal Naval Air Service.*
BENNETT, J., *Cheshire Regt.*
BICKERSTON, —, *7th Batt. Manchester Regt.*
BIANCHI, A., *Royal Engineers.*
BODEN, F., *8th Batt. Manchester Regt. (T.F.).*
BOOTH, J., *King's Own Lancaster Regt.*
BOULD, N., *Royal Scots.*
BOYLE, M., *7th Batt. Manchester Regiment.*
BRADDOCK, G., *8th Lancs. Fusiliers (Terr.).*
BRIGGS, J., *Royal Field Artillery.*
BRISCOE, D., *Royal Field Artillery.*
BUDD, C., *Army Service Corps (M.T.).*
BULLOCK, E., *13th Batt. Manchester Regt.*
BURNEY, W., *Army Service Corps (M.T.).*
BURNS, H., *Army Service Corps.*
CALDWELL, W., *8th Batt. H.S. Lancs. Fus.*
CHADWICK, H., *Army Service Corps (M.T.).*

CLANCEY, J., *Royal Engineers.*
COATES, W., *Army Vet. Corps.*
COUPE, —, *Army Service Corps.*
COPELAND, G., *Army Service Corps (M.T.).*
CROSBY, D., *Army Service Corps (M.T.).*
DANN, P. W., *Loyal North Lancashires.*
DAVIES, J., *Naval Reserve, H.M.S. "Canopus"*
DAWSON, T., *7th Batt. Manchester Regt.*
DEAN, C., *Royal Army Medical Corps.*
DEANS, J., *3rd Batt. Lancashire Fusiliers.*
DONBAVAND, J., *7th Batt. East Lancs. Regt.*
DORAN, —, *North Lancashire Regt.*
DUNN, H., *Royal Field Artillery.*
EARNSHAW, J., *Army Service Corps (M.T.)*
EDWARDS, A., *Army Service Corps.*
FEATHERSTONE, H., *8th Bt. Man. Regt. (T.F.)*
FERUSON, V., *Army Service Corps.*
FITZSIMONS, R., *Rifle Brigade.*
FRASER, A. V., *Flying Corps, Turnborough*
GARBUTT, —, *Army Service Corps.*
GILLARD, J., *8th Batt. Manchester Regt.*
GREAVES, A., *6th Batt. Cheshire Regt.*
GREEN, —, *Lancashire Fusiliers.*
GREEN, P., *Army Service Corps.*
GODDARD, Sergt. W., *11th Hussars (Res.).*

The cinema, still inscribed as 'Carlton Super Cinema' along the top and over the entrance, on Ashton New Road in Clayton (1984). Lying next to Mayne's garage and opened in the 1930s, it closed in 1964. Later it became a bingo hall and was then demolished to make way for a supermarket. Another cinema serving Clayton was just across the border in Bradford on Gibbon Street; it was named the Empress and became a billiards hall.

The Metropole theatre, showing *The Boy King*, on Ashton Old Road in Openshaw (*c.* 1914). Opened in around 1898 by William Henry Broadhead, it could originally accommodate about 4,700 people for music hall and melodrama. A steep ramp at the rear of the building led up to a pay-box and the entrance to the 'gods'. Even elephants appeared on stage. In 1938 the building was converted to a cinema, but was demolished in 1962.

The Metropole theatre, Lower Openshaw in the early 1900s. It stood on the north side of the main road, on the site of George Whyatt's dyeworks. Beyond it lay a recreation ground and then Ashton Old Road Board School on the corner of Taylor Street. On the right of it are the Thompson Drug Store Co. and a branch of William Deacon's bank, with Dyer Street, named after the dyeworks, just off the picture.

The Alhambra theatre on Ashton Old Road in Higher Openshaw (*c.* 1910). Far left lies a branch of William Deacon's bank and nearer across Old Lane, an optician and a confectionery. On the right are Syke's tobacconist shop and Redman's grocery, next to Brough (late Bank) Street. Across this street lies Fentem's bakery (a butchers in 1878), with its delivery cart. Originally, Henry Crabtree & Sons' Bank dyeworks occupied the site of the Alhambra.

BEYER, PEACOCK & CO. LTD. 1216

CENTENARY PRESENTATION
of the film
"Beyer-Garratt Locomotives in New South Wales"
with
SUPPORTING FEATURE
at
Alhambra Theatre, Higher Openshaw
SATURDAY, 26th JUNE, 1954
at 10-30 a.m.

ADMIT TWO

A ticket for the centenary film of Beyer Peacock (of Gorton) in 1954. The Alhambra theatre opened in 1909 for music hall and stage shows with an orchestra. A cinema at the rear, called the Pavilion and accessed from Buckley Street, accommodated up to 1,500. In 1916 the theatre itself became the cinema and the Pavilion a dance hall. A billiards hall existed upstairs.

Snooker players in Openshaw Liberal Club on Greenside Lane in 1969. Players are, from left to right: Charlie Dutton, James Sheldon, Rod Corfield and Dale Woolley.

The Girl Guide company of St Willibrord's Roman Catholic church in Clayton, 1956. With them is their captain, Miss E. Leadbeater and lieutenant, Miss J. Harrop. In 1955 they won the prized Bishop Casartelli Standard, awarded for attendance, smartness and turn-out at the Diocesan church parade.

The band of the Boys' Brigade of St Cross Anglican church in Clayton, accompanying a Whit Walk in the 1950s. Behind them lies the old church school building. Many churches had their own company, such as the Higher Openshaw Wesleyan church on Ogden Lane.

Above: A Whit Walk procession in the mid-1970s. The band of the Girls' Brigade of St Cross Anglican church, Clayton march along Seymour Road South and are just passing Seymour Road primary school.

Right: Colin Summer, the drum major of the band of the Boys' Brigade company of St Cross Anglican church. He leads the way past the church of St Cross on Ashton New Road.

The Boy Scouts company of St Willibrord's Roman Catholic church, Clayton in 1956, the Diamond Jubilee year of the church. With them is their Scout master, Mr W. Day. The company was founded by Mr W. Bardsley. Other churches had such a company, like St Anne's Roman Catholic church in Higher Openshaw.

Girl Guides of Cornwall Street Baptist chuch cross Openshaw Bridge on Ashton Old Road, Openshaw in the early 1960s.

Fairfield Wells House,
Higher Openshaw.

HIGH-CLASS ORCHESTRA FOR BALLS, RECEPTIONS, &C.

ALL THE LATEST DANCE MUSIC.

Sincerely yours,
L. W. EVANS.

. **Fairfield Private** .
School of Dancing.

U.K.A. DIPLOMA AND GOLD BADGE.

MEMBER U.P.T.D. AMERICA.

Yours sincerely,
F. B. EVANS.

A leaflet advertising Fairfield school of dancing at Fairfield Wells House in Higher Openshaw, Ashton Old Road (1909). Run by the Evans family, it offered private and group lessons and a private orchestra for hire. Their house was between the Empire laundry and the Washington box works. Other dance halls included the Co-operative in Lower Openshaw, the Granville above the Openshaw Liberal Club and Chick Hibbert's 'Rainbow' at the Alhambra in Higher Openshaw.

Opposite, above: George Bennett watches Colin Stott play the piano in the parish room of St Clement's Anglican church in Higher Openshaw (*c.* 1962). They were both members of the Youth Fellowship, who met here on Saturday evenings. Lying across Ashton Old Road, opposite the church, this had been the original Mission church of St Luke. Demolished in 1976, it was replaced by the old infants' school, which later became the Parish Hall. Another musical group was the Crossley girls' choir in Lower Openshaw.

Opposite, below: A school pageant at St Clement's Anglican church, Higher Openshaw, in the 1950s. They are in the main hall of the church's junior school on Ashton Old Road. From left to right, front row: -?-, Irene Phillips. Middle row: Kenneth Wright, Lawrence Booth. Back row: Pat Lever (dressed as Britannia), George Bennett.

A hiking party from the Youth Fellowship of St Clement's Anglican church out in Derbyshire (Bank Holiday Monday, August 1962). From left to right: -?-, Vivien Bown, New Zealander Owen Kimberley (Curate and leader), Alan Buckley, Barbara Bate, Dorothy Taylor, John Buckley, -?-, -?-. Other youth clubs existed, such as at Wheler Street in Openshaw.

Crossley Lads Club on their annual camping holiday, at Carnarvon in 1907. This gave city boys a holiday in the country or by the sea, but they had to qualify by doing 'useful' work during the winter. The first camp was in 1889 at Whaley Bridge. In 1892 they changed venue to Delamere for three years, followed by Morecambe, Salop and Carnarvon in North Wales, which was described as the best on record. About 300 to 500 boys enjoyed a camp gazette, competitive sports and a daily service.

The Northside Amateur Boxing Club on North Road in Clayton (2002). This was the sports pavilion of the Openshaw Crossley Lads Club. Their first ground was near Belle Vue station in Gorton. This ground, on North Road, covered seven acres and catered for football, cricket, hockey and tennis. The two-storey pavilion included showers and dressing rooms. In the 1930s the playing fields were built over, and the club moved to Melland Road playing fields off Mount Road in Gorton.

The football team of St Anne's Roman Catholic church in Fairfield were league and cup winners in the 1934/35 season. There were football teams in Clayton on the Edge Lane ground and the at Dingle, including Medlock Rovers and Clayton Methodists. In Openshaw there were, among others: Fairfield, Clarence, Wesleyan, Shop Assistants, AEU and Wheler Street youth club football teams, as well as the Ferguson baseball team.

A plaque to Charlie Roberts, centre half and captain of Manchester United football team between 1905 and 1913, and chair of the Professional Footballers' Association from 1918 to 1921. His family ran a sweet shop on the corner of Bank Street. The Newton Heath (London & Yorkshire Railway Co.) team played from 1878 near the works at North Road in Clayton. The Heathers (Newton Heath) team became Manchester United Football Club in 1901, playing at Bank Street and then in 1910 moving to Old Trafford.

The Sir Humphrey Chetham public house on Ashton New Road in Clayton (1994). A successful merchant and benefactor to Manchester, he lived at Clayton Hall (see pages 22-4). The inn belonged to Issell Taylor in the 1870s, when it boasted a bowling green, stables and 'ample grounds and pleasant harbours'. In 1924 it was bought by Chesters' brewery. Later it had its own football team, named 'Kath Rovers' after the landlady. Lying opposite Clayton Methodist church, the pub was two doors away from John Redditt's clog and boot shop (see page 76).

A Silver Wedding celebration party at the Folkestone Hotel on the corner of Folkestone Road West and Folkestone Road in Clayton, in 1968. Joan and Bill Jeffries and guests enjoy their party inside this public house, which was built to serve the large housing estate erected north of North Road by the 1930s.

The Openshaw public house on the south side of Ashton Old Road in Lower Openshaw (2002). On the left is Mitchell Street, and on the right was a branch of Seymour Mead's grocery, on the corner of Ensign (late Elizabeth) Street. In the 1870s the pub belonged to Thomas Chesters' brewery. The façade is decorated with carved heads portraying prominent Victorians. The building now stands derelict.

A Whit Walk procession passes by the Ashbury's Arms on the north side of Ashton Old Road, Lower Openshaw in 1965. This existed as a beer retailer from the 1870s, belonging to Chesters' brewery from 1891. On the right lies Taylor Street, across which lay Ashton Old Road council school and the Metropole theatre. The shop on the left of the pub was a butchers. The Ashbury's was demolished to allow road widening in 1968.

The Travellers' Call public house on the north side of Ashton Old Road in Lower Openshaw (1973). This was a Thomas Chesters' brewery house in the 1870s. Chesters gave it up in 1891, and in 1949 it came to Wilson's through a merger with Walker & Holmfray's brewery. It lay between Dyer Street and Ivy Street, where there was a corner post office, but they were all demolished for road widening.

The Star Inn on Pottery Lane in Openshaw (1991). Lying on the west side of the lane, it has Jarrold Street on the left and Huddleston Street off to the right, with Ashbury's railway station further along. This public house existed in the 1870s, and in 1903 it was bought by Chesters' brewery from John Battersby of the Wellington brewery (see pages 30 and 56).

The Church Hotel public house on the north side of Ashton Old Road, Openshaw. Lying on the corner of Clayton Lane, it was a Chesters' brewery house with Charles Frost as landlord in 1914. Mill Street is off to the left and nearby were a cycle shop and a butchers.

Above: A Whit Walk procession along the north side of Ashton Old Road and past the Legh Arms in Openshaw, during the 1950s. The public house has Dawnay (late Davies) Street on the right, with the Whitworth Hall beyond. Behind the pub lay the school of St Barnabas (see page 122). On the left was a tall building used as a funeral parlour. In the 1870s the Legh Arms was a tied house of the Swan brewery of Ardwick. Sold to Chesters' brewery in around 1890, it finally became a Whitbread brewery house.

Right: A Whit Walk procession passes along the north side of Ashton Old Road and past the Lord Wolseley public house, Openshaw in the 1950s. The public house has Wood Street on the left, with a butchers shop on its opposite corner. The Lord Wolseley existed in the 1870s, was a Chesters' brewery house from 1888 and later became known as the Queen Anne.

The Cromwell Inn public house on the south side of Ashton Old Road in Lower Openshaw. It had Wright Street on the right and Rowell (late Cromwell) Street on the left. It existed as a beer retailer in 1914. Both the public house and Wright Street were demolished in a 1968 clearance scheme.

The Drovers' Inn on the north side of Ashton Old Road, 1973. Bartlett (late Brunswick) Street lies on the right. In the 1700s it was the first building reached in Openshaw on the road from Manchester, and it was known as the 'Sheepshouters' or 'Walker's Tenement'. Later it was renamed the Drovers' Inn or 'Shouters'. Chesters bought the land from John Battersby of the Wellington brewery in 1888. The public house is now closed.

The Jolly Carter public house on the north side of Ashton Old Road, Openshaw 1973. Lying on the corner of Greenside (late George) Street, in 1872 it is recorded as trading with Hyde's Mayfield brewery in Ardwick. Up until 1914 it is listed as a beer retailer in directories. It became a Charrington's brewery house, but is now demolished.

The Pack Horse Hotel on the north side of Ashton Old Road, Higher Openshaw, 1973. Lying on the corner of Louisa Street, it existed in 1745, when James Taylor was landlord. In 1831 it was the headquarters of the Lancastrian Friendly Burial Society, the 'Neck or Nowt'. By the 1870s it belonged to Groves & Whitnall, and later Holt's brewery. Supposedly it was a stop-off point in the 1800s for wagons of prisoners, who were chained in the cellars while the warders supped.

Right: Karen Singleton with Janet Sheldon (on the right) in 1964. Karen lived at the Staff of Life public house, where her father was the landlord.

Below: The Staff of Life public house on the north side of Ashton Old Road, Openshaw, 1991. It lies on the corners of Dakely (late Grimshaw) and Silkstone (late Simpson) Streets, where George Shaw's spring works once operated. It existed in the 1870s, later becoming a Wilson's brewery house, and surviving today as a private house.

A Whit Walk procession from Cornwall Street Baptist church on the south side of Ashton Old Road, Openshaw, in the early 1960s. In the distance is the Locomotive Tavern on the corner of Cornwall Street. John Smith & Sons' ironfounders lay opposite across Cornwall Street (see page 59). The public house existed in 1872, trading with Hyde's Mayfield brewery in Ardwick. It became the Smithfield until demolition.

A Whit Walk procession on the north side of Ashton Old Road, Openshaw in the early 1960s. Behind lies the Fountain public house on the corner of Turton Street. In the 1870s it was an Openshaw's brewery house. Across Turton Street in 1965 were a hairdressers, newsagents and wallpaper shops, followed by the Droylsden Co-operative stores and then the Prince of Wales public house across Tunstall Street. Both public houses are demolished.

The Forresters' Arms on the south side of Ashton Old Road, Higher Openshaw in 2004. Lying on the corner of Erin (late Ellen) Street, it existed in 1864, trading with Hyde's Crown brewery in Audenshaw. In the 1870s it was a Groves & Whitnall brewery house, but the Atlas brewery had taken over by 1914. Finally it passed to Robinson's brewery.

The Concert Inn on Fairfield Road in Higher Openshaw, 2004. It lay on the west side of the road, opposite the Salvation Army citadel, and on the right is Buckley Street. In the 1870s it was an Openshaw's brewery house. Eventually it became a Boddington's house.

The Lord Raglan public house on the south side of Ashton Old Road, with the Halfway House public house across Ogden Lane, Higher Openshaw in the 1970s. In the 1870s the Lord Raglan was a Stopford's brewery house, but it was let to the Walker & Holmfray brewery in 1937 by the Palatine Bottling Co. and later became a Wilson's house. A Red Lion public house existed in the 1700s in Little Droylsden within Openshaw, and in 1733 it was rebuilt here between Ogden Lane and Vine Street. Its licence went to the Halfway House in the early 1800s and, when that licence lapsed in 1859, the nearby New Inn was renamed the Halfway. In 1872 the Halfway House was rebuilt, but is now renamed.

The Napoleon Inn on Cornwall Street in Openshaw (2004). On the right lies Lawton Street and on the left was a hardware dealer, next to Violet Street. It is a red-brick building with a brick extension on the left, to which this façade was added. It was a Walker's brewery house. Renamed the Jive Inn, it is now closed.

Right: Members of St
Cross Anglican church,
Clayton, in the school yard
on a Whit Walk (*c.* 1956).

Below: A Whit Walk by
members of the church of
St Cross, in the mid-1970s.
Here they are on Clayton
Street, passing
St Cross church with the
church school behind
them. The chimney
belongs to the Anchor
Chemical Co. on Clayton
Lane.

Maggie Reed standing outside her home on Hackle Street in Clayton (*c.* 1929). Aged about six, she has a flower basket next to her, ready to join in a Whit Walk with Clayton Methodist church, of Seymour Road South (see page 110).

Members of the Sunday school of the church of St Cross on North Road, Clayton on a Whit Walk in 1958. They are near St Willibrord's Roman Catholic church. The girl at the front is Barbara Sharr.

Left: Canon Buckley (on the right)
and a fellow priest take part in a
Whit Walk along North Road in
Clayton on May Sunday, 1968. They
were priests at St Willibrord's Roman
Catholic church.

Below: Members of Clayton
Methodist church of North Road
taking part in a Whit Walk in 1978.
They are lined up on North Road.

Christine Hughes, the Rose Queen of St Willibrord's Roman Catholic church, leads her retinue along Vale Road, Clayton on a Whit Walk (May Sunday 1968).

A Whit Walk procession along Ashton Old Road in Openshaw, in the late 1950s. The choir and banner of St Vincent de Paul are just passing the Lord Wolseley public house on the left.

Girls taking part in a Whit Walk along the north side of Ashton Old Road, Openshaw in the late 1950s. They have just passed the Legh Arms public house and the tall building of a funeral directors.

Members of St Clement's Anglican church in Higher Openshaw, taking part in a Whit Walk on Whit Saturday (*c.* 1953). Behind them on the right lies the rectory next to Gransmoor Road. The bell cote of the senior school is just visible behind the rectory. The boys are carrying the Sunday school banner. The Higher Openshaw Salvation Army band usually accompanied them.

Members of St Clement's church on their Whit Walk, in the 1960s. They are walking along Neston Street past Delamere Park with the houses of Oxton Street behind them.

Cornwall Street Baptists on their Whit Walk procession in the early 1960s. Notice the old public conveniences in the background.

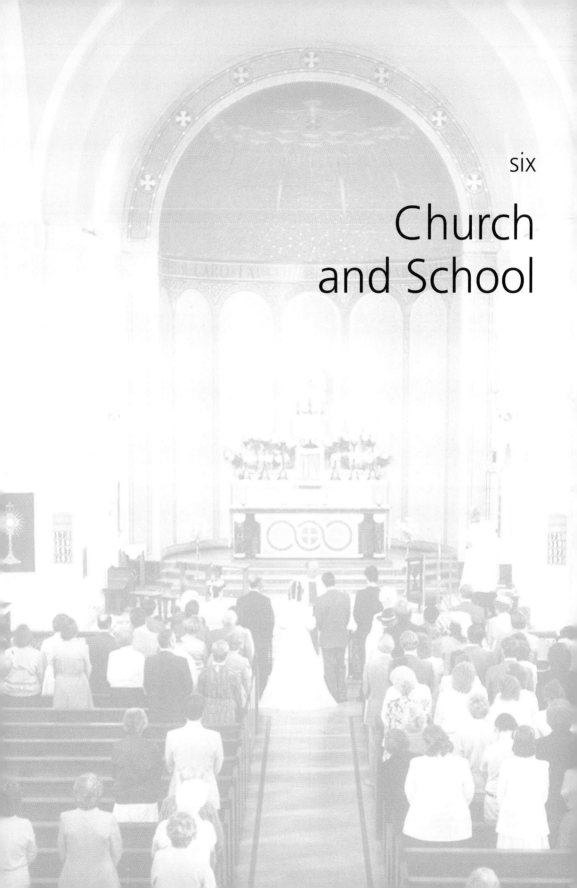

six

Church
and School

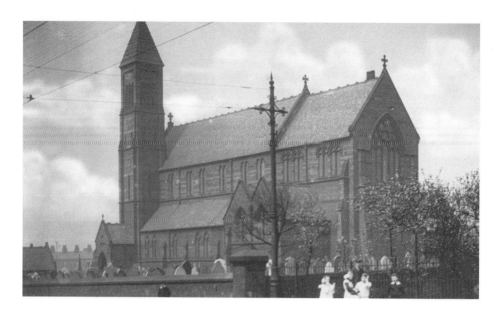

The church of St Cross, Clayton (*c.* 1910). Its land, lying on the north side of Ashton New Road, adjoining Clayton Hall and bounded by North Road and Clayton Street, was the gift of Mr C.A.R. Hoare from his Clayton Hall estate. The church, consecrated in June 1874 and designed by W. Butterfield, was finally named as St Cross after it shape. A Sunday school had preceded the church in 1854 with a school/chapel being erected in 1857.

The wedding of Jim Reed and Maggie Richardson at the church of St Cross in 1945. From left to right, back row: George Richardson (bride's brother), Joan Reed (groom's sister), Jim Reed, Maggie Richardson, Humphrey Chetham (best man). Front row: Patricia Richardson (George's daughter) and Jean Richardson (bride's niece). All the dresses were white and the flowers were tulips. The newly-weds lived on Vale Street.

The wedding of Kevan Mulqueen and Shirley Lomas at the church of St Cross, June 1967. Standing outside the church doorway are the bride and groom and their bridesmaids. Janet Sheldon, school friend of the bride, stands on the left and Jaquie and Bernadette Mulqueen, the groom's sisters, on the right.

The Marian shrine in the grounds of St Willibrord's Roman Catholic church on North Road (1968). Here the May Queen Christine Hughes and her attendants stand in front of the shrine. At Solemn High Mass on New Year's Eve in 1954, Father Buckley led a torchlit procession, including the Agnesians and the Children of Mary, to open this shrine. They concluded with the *Salve Regina* in church.

Father William Sassen of St Brigid's church arranged the first Mass in Clayton for over thirty people in Clayton House. Being of Dutch origin, he gave this church its unique Dutch dedication. Father Charles Hanrahan was the first priest in 1906 but it was his successor, Father Richard Mortimer, who in 1909 oversaw the building of a mission school/chapel, in use for twenty-nine years.

A wedding inside St Willibrord's Roman Catholic church in 1986. A plot of land was purchased on North Road and in 1937 Father Patrick Dillon led over a thousand people at the foundation service of this permanent church. Opened in 1938, this Byzantine-style building was designed by F.M. Reynolds & Scott and cost £21,000. There are three large domes over the nave, side chapels to St Joseph and Our Lady, marble altars and mosaic floors.

The team of cleaners at the church, drawn from the Women's and the Children of Mary Confraternities (1956).

Some of the gardeners of St Willibrord's Roman Catholic church (1956). Father McCormack led a team in the early days to lay out the gardens and C. Welsh, G. Carroll and the Neilson brothers continued the work in the 1950s.

The United Reformed church of St Matthew on Seymour Road, by Coatbridge Street in Clayton (2002). In 1904 the Congregationists moved here from the Co-operative hall on Ashton New Road, to a temporary chapel for 250 people and a Sunday school for 150. In 1910 they founded Clayton Congregational church here at a cost of £6,500, which in 1974 was renamed St Matthew's, combining with the Presbyterians. In 2002 they joined with Edge Lane Methodist and St Andrew's Anglican churches to become 'The Church on the Edge'.

St. Barnabus' Church, Openshaw

Left: The church of St Barnabas on South Street, Openshaw (*c.* 1908). A mission church was opened in Kay Street in Higher Openshaw in 1829, following their Sunday school (nicknamed the 'Bunghole school') in 1824 on the site of the future Ashton Old Road Board school. A permanent church, designed by Atkins and on land given by the Legh family, opened in 1839. Dry rot caused it to be demolished in 1959 and a new church was dedicated in 1962.

Below: Clayton Methodist church on the corner of Seymour Road South and North Road (2002). Over the doorway is a stone inscribed 'MNC 1905' (Methodist New Connexion). On this large site they intended to build a chapel next to this school/chapel, but this building has continued to serve as a church. In 1870 a Primitive Methodist chapel opened on Ashton New Road between Bank Street and North Road. It closed in 1963 and was demolished.

Right: The wedding of Bob Hulin and Susan Burrows inside the rebuilt church of St Barnabas (1968). At one time there was a plaque to 'Valour' from Gorton Tank on the perimeter wall of the church; it was put there when Gorton Tank closed in 1963, but was stolen in the 1970s.

Below: The wedding group at the marriage of Barry Williams and Marlene Sheldon outside the newly rebuilt Anglican church of St Barnabas on 2 September 1967. The old church originally had an 87ft-tall wooden steeple, which was dismantled in 1905.

Left: The wedding day of Leonard and Marjorie Bullock, 20 December 1952. They were married in the church of St Clement. The rector of St Barnabas in Openshaw opened a Sunday school in 1870 in the basement of four cottages on Fairfield Road, moving next into a disused workshop on Vine Street. In 1872 a school/chapel called St Luke's (or 'The Tin Tabernacle') was opened on the south side of Ashton Old Road. In 1876 a temporary iron church followed, built in front of the day school and in use until early 1881.

Below: The church of St Clement's on the north side of Ashton Old Road, Higher Openshaw (*c.* 1910). In 1876 land was given by the Legh family for a permanent church across Ashton Old Road. Money was short, but a grant was obtained from Manchester's St Clement's charity fund, and so the name was changed from St Luke's to St Clement's. The church, designed by Enticknap & Both, was consecrated in 1881 but its proposed tower was never built.

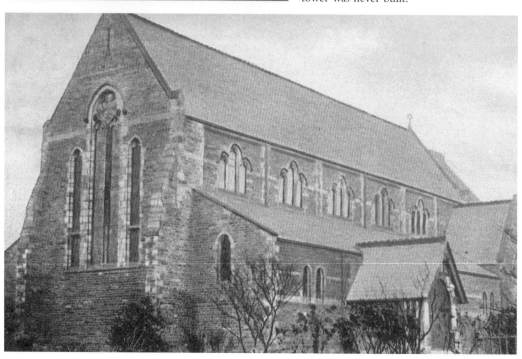

The Roman Catholic church of St Vincent de Paul on Greenside (late George) Street in Lower Openshaw (2002). The church school lies on the right. Craydon Street is off to the left, where there is the presbytery for the priest. A mission school/chapel building was founded in 1896; it was two storeys tall, with the school above and chapel below. The permanent church opened in 1905 and a new church was built in 1955, which joined with St Brigid's church in Ancoats.

Members of Cornwall Street Baptist church in Openshaw set off on a Whit Walk from their church in the early 1960s. Behind them is Whitworth Street East, leading right to Ashton Old Road. Started in a school room on that same corner in 1878, the church was built in 1906. In 1971 they reunited with the Mersey Street Baptists, who had split from them in 1922 and who had by 1926 built the Baptist Tabernacle on Mersey Street.

Left: Thomas Ashbury, author of a book about the development of Wesleyan Methodism in Openshaw (1916). A leading local Methodist attending the church on Grey Mare Lane, he had contributed £1,000 to the building fund.

Below: Openshaw Wesleyan Methodist church on Grey Mare Lane in Lower Openshaw (1916). In 1839 a school/chapel was built on the south side of Ashton Old Road. It was sold to the Congregationalists in 1864 when this new church was opened, designed by W.H. Hayley and accommodating 590 people. A day-school followed in 1865, replaced in 1872 by a new school. They were closed in 1960.

The Methodist Free church on Tipton Street in Lower Openshaw
(1891). From 1847 they met in a hatter's workshop on Wood Street. In
1860 they opened a school/chapel opposite Wood Street, and in 1864
it became Central Openshaw United Methodist Free chapel. In 1889
they opened this Early English Gothic-style church, seating 650 people.
Tipton Street church closed in 1966.

The Gransmoor Road Methodist church in Higher Openshaw (1937).
In 1839 the Moor Lane school/chapel off Fairfield Road was opened
with 450 scholars. From 1852 they were part of the Manchester South
MNC circuit and during 1903 a new school was opened on Gransmoor
Road, followed by the church. In 1917 they became part of the enlarged
United Methodist Openshaw circuit, together with Clayton MNC
Methodist church.

Higher Openshaw Wesleyan church on Ogden Lane. Erected in 1890, this chapel adjoined
the earlier school/chapel, and in 1909 a new school was added. The church was demolished
but the school still stands. Other nearby chapels included Lower Openshaw United
Methodist Free chapel on Barmouth Street, built in 1901 and demolished in 1959, and
Higher Openshaw Primitive Methodist chapel on Ashton Old Road, with a school/chapel
from 1872 and a church from 1894 until its closure in 1966.

Opposite, above: The Stanley Street school/chapel of Higher Openshaw Weslyan Methodist church, which stood from 1877 to 1908. In 1881 they extended the old infants' school and added a lecture room upstairs.

Right: The present Openshaw church of the Moravians, on Wheler Street in Higher Openshaw. The original iron mission church was founded by the Moravians from the settlement at Fairfield in 1899.

Below: Hulme Beulah Hall, on the corner of Beulah Street and Whitworth Street in Openshaw (2004). Now a paintworks, only the name and the arched windows reveal its origins as a Welsh Wesleyan chapel. An eroded sandstone nameplate adorns the doorway. A Welsh Wesleyan mission room existed in 1905 on Ashton Old Road, on the corner of Compass (late Clarence) Street, in part of the Openshaw Overseers' office building, next to the rectory of St Barnabas.

A Whit Walk procession passes by the Anglican church school of St Cross on Clayton Street in the early 1960s. From 1854 there was a Sunday school in some cottages near Clayton Hall, with services held there from 1855. The day school/chapel of St Cross was opened in 1857, built in a 'T' shape and on land provided by the Hoare family. By 1859, 123 pupils were on the register.

A section of the annual whole school photograph of St Willibrord's Roman Catholic church, Clayton (1956). Founded in 1909 and opened in 1910 with four teachers and one headmaster, Mr McElhatan, the school expanded rapidly when the housing estates of the 1930s grew up around it. The Second World War delayed extensions but by 1947 seven extra classrooms were added to the site. A new infants' school on Vale Street opened in 1973 and a junior school in 1998.

Ravensbury primary school on Ravensbury Street in Clayton (2002). Sited off Bank Street and north of Ashton New Road, this building, meant for 400 children, replaced a temporary 'tin school' in the early 1900s. It was known for its sports teams, such as 'Ravy's' football team. In 2004 this school building was demolished, as a new community primary school has replaced it.

Standard IIA of Seymour Road school in Clayton (1922). Front row second from the left sits George Richardson. The foundation stone on the front of the building reads 'This Memorial stone of the thirty third school erected by the city of Manchester School Board was laid by William Richmond Esquire, member of the board. 20 October 1900'. Another stone is inscribed 'MSB 1900'.

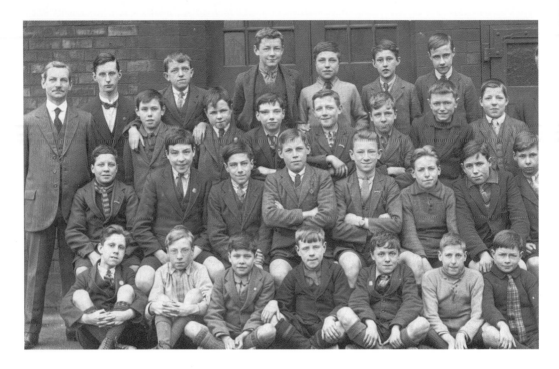

A class at Seymour Road school, Clayton (*c.* 1924). Front row third from the left sits George Richardson. The school has separate entrances for girls (on the left) and for boys (on the right), plus a separate nursery school on the right-hand side with the Manchester coat of arms adorning the building.

Standard IB of Seymour Road school in April 1934. Their teacher is Miss Brown and in the back row, second from the right, is Leonard Bullock.

'The Babies' at play in the school yard of the school of St Clement's Anglican church, Higher Openshaw in June 1926. On the left stands George Bennett (aged four). The school lay opposite the church on the south side of Ashton Old Road. The infants' playground at the back eventually became the boys' playground. The windows above the wall on the right belong to houses on Capital (late City) Road.

Dancing around the maypole at St Clement's church school, *c.* 1930. Among the infants stands George Bennett, aged about eight, in the middle at the front. Twenty years later, his son George (aged eight) also danced around that maypole. The school was opened as St Luke's in 1872 and was also used as a church. It changed its name when the church was built (see page 112).

The third-year class of St Clement's church school in 1953. On the left stands the headmaster, Mr Milne, and on the right the class teacher, Mr Raynor. Back row, first on the right, stands George Bennett. In 1899 the mixed department moved to a new home on Gransmoor Road, known as the 'Big School', until 1967, when the upper school closed and the building was then demolished. In 1978 the infants moved to new premises on Ackroyd Street.

The old buildings of St Barnabas' Anglican church school with the Legh Arms on the left on Dawnay (late Davies) Street in Openshaw, 2004. Opened in 1833 on South Street, it predated the church (see page 110). In 1877 a new infants' school was built, funded by their patron Mrs W. Brundet. The school lay to the left of the church on South Street and also opposite on Dawnay Street. In 1973 a replacement school on Parkhouse Street opened, called Openshaw Church of England primary school.

The school of the Roman Catholic church of St Vincent de Paul on Greenside (late George) Street in Openshaw (2002). Lying on the corner of North Street, the school is now closed.

The remains of the 'Tank School' (the Manchester, Sheffield & Lincolnshire Railway school) on Cornwall Street, Openshaw before demolition in 2004. Opened in 1856 for the children of railway employees, it was taken over by the Manchester School Board in 1894 and closed in 1897. It became the Staff Association Club and works canteen.

Pupils of Ashton Old Road county primary school in Lower Openshaw take part in a May Day celebration, *c.* 1960. From left to right stand Peter McGarr, John Hodson, Sandra ?, Neil Rothray, Irene Barnett, Wendy ?, –?–, David Fawley and –?–. It occupied the site of the 1824 Sunday school of St Barnabas, nicknamed 'the Bunghole school' (see page 110). It was opened in 1894 as school No. 25 by the city of Manchester School Board, and was bounded by Taylor, Whyatt and Wellington Streets and Ashton Old Road.

Opposite, above: Varna Street elementary school in Higher Openshaw (2003). Opened in 1897 as school No. 32 of the Manchester School Board, it replaced the Tank School on Cornwall Street. From 1924 until 1934 Varna Street central school occupied part of the building, but from 1934 the seniors and juniors used this school. In 1967 the seniors moved to secondary schools and the school became known as Varna Street Primary.

Opposite, below: Standard Three at Elysian Street council elementary school, Elysian Street, Openshaw in 1962. The teacher is Miss Skinner. From left to right, back row: James Carter, Billy Jones, Pamela Jackson, Susan Valentine, Jean Elliot, Jan Leonard, Christine Dugdale, Chris Williamson, David Johnson. Second row: Edward True, Wayne Hutchinson, Keith Astbury, James Leeson, Peter Lignum, Rob Godwin, Billy Brown, Alan Pace, George True, Brian Walker. Third row: Wendy Woods, Carol Langhorn, Karen Singleton, Lynn Smith, Susan Aldred, Carol Cale, Janet Sheldon, Christine Mather, Doreen Beresford. Front row: Barry Potter, Lesley Stubbs, Philip Gettings, John Needham, Graham Robinson, Colin Webb, Eric Bromley, Kenneth Taylor. The school started in a temporary corrugated-iron building in 1904 and moved to new accommodation in 1911. It was demolished in 1983.

A class in Wheler Street council school in Sandywell Street, Higher Openshaw (1902). The children had just moved in, having marched up from Varna Street elementary school. The desks and chairs are brand new, as the school had just opened. It was bounded by Old Lane and Printer Street.

Another class on the opening day of Wheler Street council school in 1902.

A class at Wheler Street infants school in 1958. From left to right, back row: Teacher, Graham Earl, -?-, -?-, Peter Delaroute, Christine Grace, -?-, Anne Bullock, Jane Leah, Teacher. Front row: Lorraine Morton, -?-, -?-, -?-, -?-, Pamela Booth, Jimmy Potter. Seated on floor: Janet ?, -?-. The school closed in 1967 and became a community centre.

Openshaw technical college on the corner of Boyd and Whitworth Streets. It opened in 1955 on the site of Joseph Whitworth's works and offered mechanical and electrical engineering courses. It was extended in 1968 to become the Openshaw Centre of the Manchester Central College, merging in 1983 to become part of MANCAT. This original building was demolished in 1996.

Other local titles published by The History Press

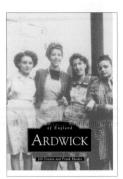

Ardwick

JILL CRONIN AND FRANK RHODES

Ardwick was one of Manchester's first suburbs and this collection of over 200 old photographs illustrates life and times in the area over a period of 100 years. In the nineteenth century the area was a desirable residential quarter for the rich. Later its character changed as it attracted industry and the cramped housing associated with it. As the area changes once again, with building clearances and new developments, this book provides a timely record of what went before.

0 7524 2473 4

Voices of Ashton-under-Lyne

DEREK SOUTHALL

These are the memories of people who have lived and worked in Ashton-under-Lyne. Together with a fascinating selection of old photographs, they paint a vivid picture of everyday life in the town throughout the twentieth century. For older readers it will be a nostalgic trip and for younger ones an insight into a world that has largely disappeared.

0 7524 2160 3

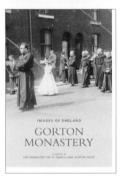

Gorton Monastery

MONASTERY OF ST FRANCIS AND GORTON TRUST

In the 1860s a group of Franciscan friars came to Gorton and established a friary and a parish church of grand proportions, built to a design by E.W. Pugin. The church was at the centre of social and religious life in Gorton for over a century but then went into decline and closed. In the nick of time a trust was set up to save the monastery from demolition and restore it. This book of photographs shows the great church in its heyday and tells the story of its route back to survival and restoration.

0 7524 3208 7

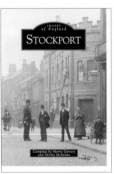

Stockport

MORRIS GARRATT AND SHIRLEY MCKENNA

This collection of 220 photographs and illustrations, many never published before, takes in the sights and scenes of Stockport and surrounding areas, including Vernon Park, Portwood, Tiviot Dale, the Heatons and Edgeley. The reader will encounter townscapes, streets and buildings such as pubs, cinemas and shops, many of which have now disappeared. These images will re-awaken memories among older residents, and show younger readers the town as it used to be.

0 7524 1128 4

If you are interested in purchasing other books published by The History Press, or in case you have difficulty finding any of our books in your local bookshop, you can also place orders directly through our website

www.thehistorypress.co.uk